T0207635

a Woman after Her Own Heart

Glenda Rose

iUniverse, Inc.
Bloomington

iUniverse books may be ordered through booksellers or by contacting:

iUniverse
1663 Liberty Drive
Bloomington, IN 47403
www.iuniverse.com
1-800-Authors (1-800-288-4677)

Because of the dynamic nature of the Internet, any web addresses or links contained in this book may have changed since publication and may no longer be valid. The views expressed in this work are solely those of the author and do not necessarily reflect the views of the publisher, and the publisher hereby disclaims any responsibility for them.

Any people depicted in stock imagery provided by Thinkstock are models, and such images are being used for illustrative purposes only.

Certain stock imagery © Thinkstock.

ISBN: 978-1-4620-7059-6 (sc)
ISBN: 978-1-4620-7060-2 (e)

Printed in the United States of America

iUniverse rev. date: 2/23/2012

Acknowledgements

Sincere thanks to everyone who contributed in many ways…knowledge, love, Celebration, dedication, patience, and love.

Dedications

To my parents, the late William T. Willis Sr. and Ola Mae Willis, thank you for Being the divine couple that allowed me to come through your loins Dad and Mom's womb.

Love always, Kai.

To my Granddaughters Destiny, Danaya, and Evenly Freeman, stay true to your dreams.

To my Grandsons Nasir, Thomas Jr. and Travis, may you be established as men of valor.

To my little friend Gensis Martinez, you are a brilliant little girl.

To my family,

Love always.

Special Dedication

To Master Prophet Bernard Elijah Jordon, a master's master, a teacher's teacher.

Thank you for teaching me that I AM.

Contents

Fragrance

The quality of being fragrant, a sweet pleasing scent. A woman is a walking fragrance. She exudes a sweet-smelling scent or a bad odor. Your scent is not determined by the scent you wear but by the substance of a woman. A woman of substance is filled with preparation, equipped ready and organized for the numerous challenges that will more than likely arise in her life.

The sweet fragrant woman shows herself agreeable. There is a pleasant scent to the power of agreement. It is a scent of graciousness and allows a woman to be pleasantly kind and courteous. This characterizes good taste, comfort, ease, and mercy along with compassion. These qualities match the qualities of our King of Kings. Your fragrance ultimately brings a harmonious scent to the people you are interacting with. Your disposition can and will alter your spirit, emotions and moods. The fragrant woman must be predominantly positive and pleasant as often as possible. Your scent places you in an atmosphere of other positive or negative scents, depending on your attitude. You have heard this cliché before: "her attitude stinks". This means that your attitude is unbearable to smell. It is foul. Eventually, everyone must leave your presence. However, you can transform an unbearable attitude. First, become aware of the things that you are currently experiencing in your life. Sometimes life's circumstances will create unpleasant atmospheres. Second, make a list of your relationships, both male and female, that you could qualify through association. If their fragrance is not a desirable aroma, delete them from your guest list. Read material that positively keeps you thinking good thoughts and positive affirmations. Of course, the Bible is a sweet-smelling fragrance, so be sure to include that among your collection. Last but not least, ask for forgiveness for being such a little stinker to yourself and everyone else. As always, allow the Spirit to lead you and finish the beautiful work that has begun in you!

*Every woman has her
own designer fragrance,*

*It's called
Quality.*

I Remember

Remember when we were little girls and played in our mothers' clothes and jewelry? We put on her high heel shoes to emulate a woman. Make-up was never used to cover blemishes; it was strictly for enhancing our beauty. It made us feel like a lady. I distinctly recall the baby dolls I used to talk to, instructing them what the plans for the day would be. I read them fairy tales and brushed their baby fine hair. I made sure that my dolly was clean and smelled like Ivory soap. Boy! Oh Boy! I was a mother that beat all mothers. I proceeded to take my baby for an afternoon walk with a beautiful stroller of my day, all day long if I was allowed. I played a mother to several baby dolls. Even during meal time, I held them close to me and watched over them so they did not make a sound. These baby dolls were always well cared for, loved and nurtured. Remembering those days and becoming a mother was a prize; it was what I looked forward to and hoped for. The role models of my day were mothers in our neighborhood

4

who watched over other mothers' children. They were mothers like Ms. King on our block, Aunt Francine, who I discovered as an adult, was not my blood Aunt. Aunt Francine took my brothers and my sister and I to the movies, she babysat and, she took us to the Catholic Church. I loved lighting those candles. Still, to this day, I light the candles at the Catholic Church on 32nd street in Manhattan. I have Aunt Francine to thank for the memory of connecting God to the light.

For me, Ms. King had become the Grandmother I had never had. Dr. Berta Bell and Sissy Bell were big sisters to my sister and me. These women were our neighbors in Camden, New Jersey. Memories of playing with my dolls remind me of all of the things that I was taught along the way. Remembering my childhood is a constant reminder of how I perceived motherhood to be back in those days. Motherhood was an honor, a status in the community and a model for our neighborhood and society.

I remember!

A Mother is an honor.
She is a model for of our past,
present and future!

*Models for My Past,
Present and Future*

Thank you

Ola Mae Willis, My Mother, teacher, friend and mentor

Aunt Tot, The conversationalist

Aunt Rose, One of my favorite Aunts

Aunt Lee, Poured into my spiritual life

Aunt Margaret, Another favorite Aunt (she makes good homemade biscuits)

Aunt Love, Bold, free-spirited

Aunt Lula, A Mother's Mother

Aunt Porta, Had a huge farm, cotton field, spring water, cows, horses, and pigs. I learned our history every summer. My Grandparents were share croppers.

Aunt Mattie, Lived in walking distance to school and our home. We could visit any time.

Aunt Clara, Vibrant always, fun and positive

Nita, Jackie, Muff, Sandy and Tina, These are all my cousins who babysat me and my siblings. We always had a blast. Nita was the strictest of all of them!

To all of the Mothers in passing, who corrected us and even told On us (trust me, we got a whipping too) when we misbehaved.

Thank you for being the memory that makes me who I am today. A mother, role model, a minister, a sister, a friend a wife, a Queen!

Journal Pages, Pillars of Your Past, Present and Future

～W～

The mothers, mentors and teachers who made you Who you are today!

Pillars of Your Past, Present and Future

_____

_____

_____

_____

_____

_____

_____

_____

_____

_____

_____

_____

_____

_____

_____

_____

_____

_____

Pillars of Your Past, Present and Future

Every Now and Then

A Woman after Her Own Heart
Must have fun, excitement, indulge and
Break the cycle of seriousness
for just a moment.
Recapture your youthfulness,
playfulness and live in
The whimsical moment of time.

Instruments of Beauty

Flowers

Children at Play

A Warm Hello

A Beautiful Picture

A Manicured Lawn

Snow Falling from the Sky

A Blue Ocean

Ducks Floating in a Pond

Two Puppies at Play

Lovers Holding Hands

The Elderly Telling Stories

Watching your Favorite Movie

Good Old Southern Hospitality

Well Mannered Children

Finger Painting

Mountains

A Handsome Gentleman

An Attractive Lady

Beautiful Luggage

People Jogging

A Beautiful Smile

Painted Toes

A Walk in the Park

A Cruise

Charming Conversation

Nature

The State of Grace

The Sound of a Saxophone

A Lighted Candle

The Sun

The Moon

A Romantic Evening

Instruments of beauty are the
simple things for our pleasures.
They are the tools and organs
that work together for
A grand performance
Called Happiness.

Ladies First Worldwide Seminars, Inc.

⌒✍⌒

Monthly seminars hosted.
Check for seminars near you!
Ladiesfirstseminars.com
ladiesfirstworldwide@gmail.com

Ladies First World Wide Seminars will bring women into a spiritual oasis. While we create and develop new seminars, coach, image consultant with keen prophetic insight, Glenda K. Freeman will transform your life.

She is fun, provocative, and passionate about making positive changes to achieve higher consciousness. Too often we lose ourselves by not knowing ourselves. It is easy to get lost in a mind crowded with everyone's cares. She will amazingly surprise you with her savvy workshops, her coffee house seminars and well....why don't you join us and see for yourself.

Ladies First Is A Part Of You!

The Prophet and the Widow Woman and Dorothy

*H*aving a prophetic voice in your life is like having a life line. It is an invisible rope to climb towards your goals and dreams that have lingered in the heavens, waiting for you to grab hold and head toward the high call of achievement, purpose and destiny. I would like to introduce you to three women, used these principals to live and reach their destiny by sowing and reaping.

You may or may not have heard of the first woman. Her name was never stated. She was known as the Widow Woman of Zaraphate (1st Kings 17:10-16). Elijah, the Prophet of God, was sent to her by God so that she could sustain him. Imagine that! She was in need yet she had to sustain God's servant. Famine was in the land, and she had just enough to make two small pancakes for her and her son. The plan was to eat their last meal and die. Suddenly, the prophet Elijah shows up in her camp and requests that she bring him a cake and some water. She informed him of her poor status, yet he still commanded her to do as he said. This woman knew she was in the company of a prophet. She further knew to humble herself and obey simple instructions. Had this woman been disobedient to the voice of God through his servant, her plan to die would have been successful. Instead, a plan of intervention came to deliver her if she followed simple instructions. I am sure that much to everyone's surprise; she was sustained through supernatural supply and was back on her feet. In a matter of an hour or so, her life changed from poverty to wealth.

Let us move on and meet Dorothy. Who among us doesn't know Dorothy from Kansas, the classic story of The Wizard of Oz! Do you recall that right before the journey to the Land of Oz, Glenda the good witch came to Dorothy to point the way? She gave Dorothy detailed instructions to "Follow the yellow brick road." Yellow is the color of change and transition. She also gave Dorothy a pair of shiny red shoes which symbolized power and authority. So off Dorothy went to find the place of discovery, the Land of Oz (the place of fulfillment). During Dorothy's travels she met three friends, the Scarecrow, the Tin Man and the Lion. All of them had an urgent need. The Scarecrow lacked wisdom, the Tin Man was seeking love and the Lion was a coward. All of his life he was in need of courage. Dorothy briefed her new friends about this land and the assured promise of fulfillment. So off they went in pursuit of happiness.

Dorothy was not selfish; she was tied to her needs while focusing on the needs of others. Little did she know she was creating her miracle through servanthood? They arrived at the planned destination, having survived all of the challenges it took to get what they so desperately desired. The question arose, what about you, Dorothy? We all received what we came for, but how will you get home? Suddenly, Glenda, the good witch, appeared. (Don't you just love those "suddenly's"!) Now, before I continue, let me ask this question: did Glenda really look like a witch to you in the movie? NO! Not at all! So let's give Glenda her real title, Prophetess Glenda. Prophetess Glenda reappeared to give Dorothy her final instructions, just as Elijah appeared to the widow woman.

Let's review. When Dorothy followed her first set of instructions, her obedience allowed her to receive the second set of instructions. Dorothy had a need as well as the others, but before it could be met, she had to sow a resurrection seed of time, determination, knowledge and direction. Dorothy took her three friends to the next level. She created her miracle through servanthood just like the Widow Woman from Zaraphate-same principle, different form. Dorothy had to demonstrate God through wisdom, love and courage. When the assignment had been completed, Prophetess Glenda unlocked the mystery. Dorothy had God's power and authority all along but couldn't utilize it until she sowed. Nothing leaves heaven until something leaves the earth! Dorothy was being trained in leadership. She was walking out the principle of seed time and harvest (Pretty are the feet of them who carry the word). When Dorothy clicked her heels together three times, she had finished the course in miracles. Three miracles for three people and three clicks of the heels finalized the lesson. Dorothy landed back home, resurrected into full consciousness of I am. She gave birth to truth and identity. She became whole; nothing missing, nothing broken.

These two women represent the single woman. Your baby's daddy may be physically alive but he may be a dead beat dad. For some married women the marriage has been dead for years. This leaves her in the same situation as the Widow Woman of Zaraphate, with a dead relationship. You need a Prophet or Prophetess in your life to live again. You may have to go on a journey as Dorothy did to find your realities and possibilities. You may even have to help someone in order to be helped. You, my sister, may have to create a miracle to receive a miracle. As you can see, we are all connected with the same problem in different forms and with potential and possibilities for growth.

You must locate the prophetic voice God has assigned you. The prophetic voice is your life line out of famine and death. It is your pathway to change and transition. Single women, you are the most fortunate. You are married to God (Isaiah 54:5). You can redesign your life. You don't have to wear a pair of tight red shoes (they looked like they were killing her feet!). You don't have to ask permission to sow. You have no dead beat husband hanging around, blocking your seeds. Listen for the instructions that enable you to create your desired outcome.

*There's no place like
Success.
Is there a Prophet or
a Prophetess in your life?*

Lesson One: The Renegade Woman

How do you define this beautiful person, so fabulous on the outside but rebellious to the core on the inside? She goes from house to house gifted, anointed and knowledgeable about many things.

Her spirit is out of control. Her mind has exalted itself over everyone and she cannot be taught or tamed. She is a rebel in her own right. She resists authority. Her resistance is organized with topsy-turvy rules established by her own government of rebellion. This woman shows up in many establishments, ready to overthrow, out rule and even mutiny against authority. This woman is armed and dangerous; she will sabotage the powers and rejoice in the greatest undermining schemes. She will generally camouflage herself as a brilliant worker and supporter of the household of Faith. On the corporate end, she is the office gofer, willing to sacrifice and give her all and more. Ms. Renegade will always seek the highest levels of leadership. She will pretend and bend over backwards so she can gain entrance to your inner circle of family and friends. She smiles and works side by side with you until one day you look up and see that her hair style is quite similar to yours and, coincidently, so is her suit. Then, when you least expect it, she is secretly speaking to your staff in your tone. In many ways, she has become you.

The renegade, rebellious woman has a good eye for copying and stealing your prize possessions, if allowed. Do not fear what she does not realize. Like David and Saul in the Bible, David did not try on King Saul's armor because it would have crushed him. He was not able to carry a kingly anointing at that time, he was now grooming for the position. David was wise; she is not. Ultimately she becomes crushed and disfigured; she is noticeably exposed.

The sad ending of the story of the renegade woman is that she lost so much time on rebellion and mutiny that she failed to discover her own self worth, her purpose and her inner and outer abilities. She has missed her destiny over and over again, toying with time and lifetime opportunities that were created just for her. Shun rebellion. See it for what it is and deal with it accordingly. If this woman is you, handle it. What you don't deal with now will deal with you later.

A Woman After Her Own Heart
will deal with hidden secrets and thoughts.

Becoming a woman of character
brings you into places you so desire,
without having to commit mutiny.

What if God did not exist?

What if God did not exist?

What if God did not exist?

What if God did not exist?

What if God did not exist?

What if God did not exist?

What if God did not exist?

What if God did not exist?

What if God did not exist?

What if God did not exist?

What if God did not exist?

What if God did not exist?

What if God did not exist?

What if God did not exist?

What if God did not exist?

EXACTLY!!

Masturbation

A topic no one wants to address but one that should be openly discussed with an ear to hear; not judge. Throughout the years, I have heard several takes on the subject. Some feel as though if they cannot have sex until marriage that at least they can take care of their needs through masturbation. Scientifically, it is encouraged to relieve ones tension or desire. I read an article where the woman's doctor encouraged this practice to keep her in a happier mood.

On a spiritual level, we know there can be other things attached to masturbation. Women who are spiritual, masturbating will affect your anointing. Anyone or anything that is used by God must stay pure. You must elevate your mind from a lower nature to your highest good. As you elevate in consciousness, the thoughts may come every now and then but it will not cause you setbacks, you will conquer it with one elevated thought. Think of things that are pure and lovely and of a good report. Let's not forget that some people are challenged more than others, but as you clean out the dark places in your mind, you must be prepared with solutions to overcome! Which is your acknowledgement, reading the Word of God, meditation and feeding your soul with rightful thinking? Last but not least, purchase some lavender and go to sleep!

Sleep well!

Slave Girl

⌒✦⌒

*O*nce upon a time there was a beautiful slave girl; however, she was unaware of her beauty. She worked hard all of her life but never managed to get anywhere. She married and raised her children but her husband never saw her value. To him, she was just a slave girl. The marriage dissolved but the slave girl continued to marry into the same situation and circumstances. She just couldn't break away from bondage. Slavery became her past, present and her future.

The slave girl was given a tiara one day. She looked at it and tucked it away. She was unaware that the princess in her had arrived and the tiara was an outward representation of who she really was. She looked at the tiara many times but still missed its true meaning. Years went by and many changes had taken place. The slave girl had some good experiences, some better than others, yet they were all leading toward her purpose. Even her experiences in the fields were working for her good. As slave girl journeyed, the princess inside of her made her aware of her inner beauty, which she came to recognize as her outward beauty! That alone provoked a new hope and outlook for the slave girl. She began to realize that she had left her self worth, dignity and hope in each field she slaved in. The slave girl wanted it back so she began to pray that God would restore her; and He did. The slave girl regained her memory and began to write her own story.

That slave girl was me and today I write my own story of hope and renewal with every slave girl in mind, for those who missed the years and seasons to live as a princess. Living as a princess in your early years teaches confidence, self-worth, self-esteem, manners, protocol, etiquette and most of all self love. Sometimes we are taught those things in some form but if your confidence in yourself is too low, you will not achieve the benefit of your training. Throughout the years I went from a slave girl to a princess and today I rise to queenship. Nothing in me will ever devalue the gem that I am. For those of you who are still in the consciousness of a slave girl, you must pray that there will be a lifting of your thoughts; a total transformation must take place, and you must forgive yourself for the captivity you have placed yourself in. Remember, Queens write their own story!

Today my story is from Slave Girl to queenship. The fields that bound me are the fields that freed me. I am no longer a slave but a vessel of honor.

A Woman After Her Own Heart

will recognize that the things that bind
are the very things that set her free!

Journal Pages, Writing Your Own Story (Queenship)

I am writing my own story… Queenship

I am writing my own story… Queenship

Ladies First Products

scape By: Glenda Rose...A Women's place of relaxation, this single CD is a 25 minute relaxation power nap. It can be used for easy listening or at dinner with someone special. Escape is jazzy and soothing. Enjoy the precious moments of relaxation!

A women's journey...this CD is a collaboration of spoken word and poetry. This CD will encourage and lift your spirit.

Featured Tracks:
- Growing Up
- Forgiveness
- Beauty

Books By Glenda Rose:
- *A Woman After Her Own Heart*
- Release Date January 12, 2012
- *Recipes for Life*

To order or contact....ladiesfirstworldwide@gmail.com or visit Ladiesfirstseminars.com

Sultry Me

*M*y passion is greater than ever. After a forty-year identity drought can you blame the fire and the "excuse me, I don't care anymore" attitude. I am just doing me. Is that some type of slang or new world order to just do you? Excuse me again, sir, today is uniquely special.

The sultry woman that I am just paid me a visit and she is here to stay. This passion is pure and just. It is the passion of discovery and fulfillment of creation: created to be woman, created to be beautiful, created in wisdom, created to love and created to teach others how to be mothers, daughters, sisters and friends. Created to create; created by greatness. Therefore, I am great. Excuse me, sir; I just can't stop being Sultry Me!

Passionate about life!

A Woman After Her Own Heart
will embrace her life with passion.

*Do not make any excuses or apologies
about your discovery!*

Unequally Yoked

$\sim$

$\mathcal{P}$eople outside of the church are more yoked than most in the household of faith. I know this command was given to the household of faith, but many outsiders have followed this principal successfully.

Years ago, if a man was saved or born again (old school terminology) that was a criterion and down the aisle they went only to find out they really were not equally yoked. Let's review.

Non-believers marry within their circle of consciousness. Doctors marry in the medical field most often. Professionals marry within their professional circle.

Their idea of success brings them on one accord because their standard of success is basically the same. They understand what it took to make it happen. The hours of study, the sacrifice, and the cost. The bank loans they still have to pay back. In other words, they are on the same page.

When we are already spiritual and living in a kingdom, we must marry someone complementary to our anointing as well as education. When a woman has a heavy anointing and an in-depth ministry, she must marry someone with equal anointing or higher. If she marries lesser she must step down to his place of anointing and authority in order to become equally yoked. If he marries someone with a lesser anointing, he must groom her to raise her up to his consciousness. It may seem unfair but Boaz is the mentor.

Example:

Although Tarzan was limited in his speech, "Me, Tarzan, You Jane", Jane helped him build his vocabulary and etiquette, but he was master and king of his domain. He trained her how to live in his world as opposed to living in hers. Depending on which episode you saw, Jane was a city girl who came to the jungle. She packed her clothes and relocated to the jungle. She stepped down that luxury to primal living.

Remember King Kong? He could not survive in the world of the screaming blonde, he loved. He tried to keep her in his world but she refused. He was taken to her domain but could not survive human conditions. He lost his power because he stepped out of the kingdom God gave him. His choice for a wife, although, beautiful, was not suitable. They were unequally yoked. Even with great persistence to keep her, he was defeated in her world. As beautiful and powerful as Oprah Winfrey is, who wants to be Mr. Winfrey?

Not to mention the great singer who married out of her league into a world of other women, drugs and drama.

She was a star in her world and throughout the years she was noted as an iconic drama queen.

And let's not forget the brilliant actress who married the heavy metal guy at a pivotal point of her career. When he selfishly created a scandal, she quickly moved on and continues in her career.

Green Acres was a comedy show that demonstrated two life styles, two types of consciousness that came together. He was a farmer. She was wealthy heiress who lived on 5th Avenue, Eva Gabor. She wanted him to live in New York. He flatly refused, so she moved to his farm. She entered into his world physically but never mentally. Eva Gabor dressed every day like a model while he wore his overalls. He came home for dinner but she did not prepare meals. She was use to having a chef. Once she boiled water but the pan burned.

Although, Green Acres was very funny, it projected a thought that opposites attract, and you cling to your world and still marry into a completely different one. For those of you who remember the show, he was always cleaning up her mess. She made decisions but she knew nothing about farming. There was constant conflict in the way things were done. Actually, the show revealed what happens when we are unequally yoked! Conflict.

I have learned that if he doesn't rise to the expected level needed to maintain where you are in life, wait for the transition even in dating or it will create notable setbacks in your finances, time and productivity. In the end you lose more. Water seeks its own level. When it cannot, expect violations.

Equally yoked means on all levels, consciousness it determines everything else. Although opposites do attract, they still must be equally connected in consciousness.

Often it's women who pay a painful price to learn a tedious lesson.

Equally yoked means our minds are one!

A Woman After Her Own Heart
Will seek her level of growth
and consciousness.
She will seek potential in its highest form.

Pink Roses

~

Change the atmosphere of a room, filling it with love and success. The sunshine of beauty saturated by a fragrance will undoubtedly train your mind to love. Pink roses take you into a realm that can only be defined by each individual who travels there. Created by the personal imagination of self, you can find peace, the outlet from the chaos.

A rose is still a rose but the hidden beauty behind it remains unseen until you create it.

A Woman After Her Own Heart
Will love the sweet scent of
Pink!

Fashioned By His Love

designer finds the best fabric for the creation he or she has in mind. The designer carefully cuts out the pieces of pattern with a sharp eye for excellence so that everything is precise. The wonderful pieces are sown together and now the fabric takes on a form of a garment/dress with a high collar, long sleeves and embellished pockets with a deep hem.

The designer admires and loves his work. His creation takes form with a particular gender in mind. When the garment is completed he gives it to the woman, who has been fashioned for the assignment.

When God calls us into a status/ or position, He creates a garment that is suited for the individual. The embellishment represents the vast gifts, anointing and talents we will obtain. While wearing the garment, the deep hem allows time for us to experience growth and the deeper things of God. The sleeves cover and strengthen. The high collar is the status of priesthood fashioned in royalty, righteousness, love, peace and all the components and characteristics of the creator. This means you are going to a higher place in thoughts, deeds and work. We are so special that God has designed a garment for each and every one of us.

Let's rejoice and honor one another for our unique style and royal status of queenship. Remember, you must grow into your garment. However, it is an exclusive design made for your growth. The splendor of being an original is yours.

Embrace it!

A Woman After Her Own Heart

*Will recognize the love God
Has for her stitch by stitch!*

April's Love

⌒ᴍ⌒

1987...... Sunny California was not so sunny and bright for me. Alone and away from my family and friends, I could not justify it. I just knew this was a part of the journey. My husband and I relocated, seeking a new experience and employment while securing our commitment to love one another. I came later to complete the vision and hope for a new beginning. I decided to get one of the notorious curls that everyone was wearing, "the California Curl". I had envisioned long, large curls for my extra-long hair. At that time in my life it had grown quite long and healthy. My theory was it would save me time and money and it would be easy to maintain. Excited. Today is my hair appointment. The process begins. By the end of the day, my hair began to come out in clumps and my jet black hair was now red and over processed and border line bald. I went to another stylist who confirmed my over processed curls and cut the curls out to try to save some hair for a short cut that would have to be maintained weekly. Much to my surprise that sudden weight gain I was experiencing … you got it…. I was pregnant and losing my hair.

Here, I was in sunny California, where women roller blade in thongs and work out for breakfast, lunch and dinner, and 3,000 miles away from home. After a series of mishaps, I was slightly depressed by morning sickness. I would lay in bed, hoping for a new experience. The sun intruded my room while I was having my daily pity party. The blinds were closed but the sun truly spoke to me without saying a word. My husband, at that time, was at work and today was our anniversary! Prompted to go to lunch, by the brightness of the sun, I jumped up out of bed. I spent 2 ½ hours in preparation. Generally a makeup job takes me 8 minutes tops, a hair style 5 minutes, getting dressed maybe 30 minutes, but not this time. Remember, to me, my looks had been altered. So, trying to recapture my old self took time. Little did I know, at that time, I was going through a transformation? Wigs in the eighties were not like they are today. As I prepared, I began to feel somewhat better. I put on my favorite canary yellow linen jacket with a white silk blouse and white linen pants. I looked pretty good, so I thought! As I was walking out of the complex, a little girl stopped me with a startling comment. "Uh, you're ugly!'. Stunned I answered, "That's not nice!" She replied, "But, it's true!" I could not believe a little girl could make me so furious while feeling so much pain. You see it had only been weeks since I was healing from the same comment my husband made when he saw me in my transformation state!

At that very moment, I felt like retreating back to my room with the shades down where I felt safe but I made it to my car with the little girl walking behind me, taunting me. Pulling myself together, I said to her, "What's your name, honey?" She replied, "April, what's yours?" We ended the conversation by exchanging names and I pulled off.

During lunch, I sat at the table, unable to shake the idea of being bald, overweight and feeling ugly, unloved and wondering why I was in California. I went window shopping and returned home to retrieve my place of self-pity.

Weeks went by as I returned to my depression. One evening, I decided to sit on the patio and watch my son play happily with his new friends. Guess who walks by me and decides to stop and say hello.... April, the girl who had added to my already shattered emotions.

That day was the beginning of a friendship with a little girl who lived in a restricted environment similar to mine but mine was self-induced. Although, she was clean, her clothes were a little shabby.

"Hello April".

"Hi, what's your name again?"

"Glenda", I responded as she made her way toward me. Our conversation was different this time. She was pleasant.

"What's your favorite color? she asked and that's how our conversation started. We talked about dolls and I shared snacks with her as well as with the other children. I was known for having them by the neighborhood children. Every now and then, a family member would check on April and to make sure she was okay.

April and I began building a friendship. I discovered through a neighbor that she had been removed from her parents' home through child services. Sometimes, days would go by before she would reappear.

"Today, I will teach you how to play jacks", April. Once I noticed a gash on her head. When I asked about it, her response was, "The hard things are hard to remember". It wasn't until later that I got what she meant. The harsh things in life she consistently blocked out from memory.

Spending time with April made me realize she was me and I was her. April could not yet do anything to change her situation, but I could change mine. I could block out my memories by hiding in that room with a remarkable amount of self- pity. I could come out and face my fears. April had a low self-esteem and so did I, and because of that issue, she was critical and so was I. I hid low self-esteem behind make-up and a decent shape. April covered hers by choosing not to remember. I moved away from my mother and father. April had been forced to move. I was hurting inside and so was April. Our paths were meant to cross to console one another and reflect an image of change. The child in me was April and the woman April would grow to be was me. Still hurting from childhood experiences, never seeing my true beauty, April was my inner beauty. Her innocence, golden blonde hair, and bright blue eyes, symbolized inner peace. She had become the self-therapy I needed to heal and recover.

We spent time together. I even brought her a couple of outfits and gave them to her grandparents. April became my ministry without me knowing it, ministry for hurting women. Little did I know that pain could start at that age or even at birth? April was eight years old and in pain. Days, weeks and months went by as April became, my first daughter and my first ministry. For the first time I felt I had purpose and potential. It also became clear to me why I was in California. This was my Egypt. It was there I learned how to deliver and bring someone out of bondage. It started with me!

April had an accident months later. She was burned. The day I watched them bring her out on a stretcher, I silently wept inside. She was alive but experiencing pain in another form.

I never saw her again and was unable to find out her whereabouts. The family moved and that was the beginning of the new and the ending of the old. Thank you, April. Many times in my heart, I have thanked you. Although, we never saw one another again, I see you in some form in every woman I minister to; the little girl in every woman who cries for love, attention, healing, self-worth and acceptance.

1987 is a reflection, I will always remember!

Reflections to Remember

Reflections to Remember

Ladies First Worldwide

Seminars Inc.

~

The reinvention of a woman
Come meet Glenda Rose as she
teaches with style and grace.
Every woman must return to her garden daily
for planting, pruning, growth and creativity.

In our garden, we nurture and rejuvenate.
The splendor of being a woman
is valued and treasured.

Ladiesfirstseminars.com
Visit a seminar near you!

Thoughts of Healing

May you take the time to heal, recover, relax, rest and restore.

Healing is the children's bread. When I think of bread, I think of wealth, supply and plenty. Growing up, there was always bread in our home in the form of flour, biscuits, cornmeal, frozen dough or a loaf of bread. Whatever the form, we had a supply.

I believe that just as there are many forms of bread, there are vast forms to heal. You can be healed through medicine, supernaturally, herbs, holistic recipes, love, meditation, and yoga. Even a man's best friend, a dog, can assist in our healing.

Heal me, oh Lord, through your vastness. Teach me to identify the forms of your healing power!

Affirmations for Healing

Affirmations for Self-Esteem
I love myself

Affirmations for Life
I trust the process of life
All I need is taken care of
I am safe

Affirmations for Old Problems
I release the past.
I am free to move forward
with love in my heat.

Affirmations for Leg Problems
I move forward with confidence and joy,
knowing what is well in my future.

Affirmations for Decision Making
I am a decisive person.
I follow through and support myself with love
Affirmations for Knee Problems
I am flexible and following

Affirmations for Legs
I experience life as a joyous dance

Affirmations for Weight Gain
I am at peace with my own feelings
I am safe where I am
I create my own security
I love and approve of myself

Affirmations for Hip Problems
I am in perfect balance
I move forward in life with ease
and with joy at every age

Healing Scriptures

Psalm 103:3-4
Praise the Lord O my soul and
forget not all His benefits
Who forgives all sins and
heals your diseases

James 5:14-15
Is any of you sick. He should call on the
elders of the church to pray over him
And anoint him with oil in the name of the
Lord and the prayer offered in faith will make
The sick person well. The Lord will raise him
up. If he has sinned he will be forgiven.

3John2

Dear friend, I pray you will enjoy good
health and that all may go well with you
Even as your soul is getting along well.

Exodus 23:25
Worship the Lord your God and His
blessings will be on your food and water.
I will take away sickness from among you.

To The Mother who's Sons Rebelled

Stop blaming yourself dear, heart. Where he is now and what he is doing must be addressed through prayer, faith, seed time and harvest. Many mothers are single parents, who have been left holding down the fort while working and raising the children alone. Raising sons alone, especially today, is a tall order. When you get your sons through middle and junior high school (8th grade) congratulate yourself; 9th through 12th you might want to take go on a vacation as a reward and if they go to college and graduate, it's you who need the car so you can pack your bags and move on to the next phase of your life.

To you mother, I salute you. To the mothers whose sons did the opposite of their training, stop holding you guilty as charged. Charge yourself to move on to help the same society that fashioned your sons. You see the pitfalls, yes you do! Help another mother to avoid them. To my fellow colleagues, mothers, you have done what we knew to do. Rise up awaken your stiff bones and body broken with each pain your sons have caused. God, our Father, forgives them for they know not what they have done. They did not understand the purpose of motherhood because father was not there to demonstrate her importance.

The Father in heaven wants you to sing, O barren woman; you who have not borne the expected. Break forth into singing and cry aloud. Your season is about to drastically change. The favor of the Lord is upon you. Even the death of the sons shall be restored to you through other sons and their existence shall not be in vain. You have not been forgotten, nor the lives of your loved ones, saith the Lord. Monuments and foundations will come forth in their honor. You shall live and live again.

Fret not yourself over the evildoers for they will soon be cast down. Even the people who were in office who could have changed the situation or judged it properly will now sit in your seat for it will be you who will comfort and intercede for the unrighteous judge. Cheer up, old woman; be glad, young mothers; rejoice, women, in the household of faith. You shall see my right hand move on your behalf. For now it is your time to sing and so shall you be heard. Rejoice again. I say rejoice. You shall live again. Selah!

A Woman After Her Own Heart
Will rejoice in the prophetic utterance
As it pertains to her. Even now feel the
good tidings of restoration in your heart!

Rejoice

Rejoice

_____

_____

_____

_____

_____

_____

_____

_____

_____

_____

_____

_____

_____

_____

_____

_____

_____

_____

_____

The Perfect Shoes

***

"May I help you?" "Yes, can you please show me a size eight in a brown leather pump?" Now that I have my ideal pump in hand, let me see how it feels on my feet. Mmm, this is not a good fit. I love the shoe but it's too narrow. "Let me try the black patent leather in an 8 ½. Now, this shoe feels great, looks great, the sole of the shoe is well made, the cost indicates quality material, the brand speaks for itself, but I still want to make sure this is what I really want. I'll be back. I am going to look around a little longer. Thank you."

People and shoes have a lot in common. When a woman purchases a pair of shoes, we shop long and hard. We examine the foundation, the support of the shoe, and we love to go brand-shopping. Shop at the best stores in town and even then we may hesitate before taking the leap of faith to pull out the credit card and make the purchase official. Shoes are an external covering of beauty in different styles, colors, prices, sizes, and widths, protecting our feet while making a fashion statement.

When dating and waiting for the right companion, is it safe to want the same sturdy covering you look for in a shoe that you apply to your relationship? Sounds strange? Think about it! I've seen women, including myself, search for the perfect shoe and return shoes until the right style appears in the inventory. We just won't settle for the second best shoe! Throughout the years, I have developed a shoe mantra that applies to my potential companion. I like to wear loafer, when I am relaxed and laid back. Sandals are chic and cool and fun to wear. My sneakers provide good solid form that allows me the flexibility and balance to run. My high heels give me the lift I need from time to time and my stretch boots cover me from the harsh seasons; they protect my feet and legs and cover me through the unexpected climate changes. The color spectrums, price ranges and styles are endless. I love the variety and grateful that I have so many choices.

The ideal guy for me is just like my shoe selection. He should be able to relax and have fun. Play hard without being a loafer. I adore chic and cool with firm foundation. He firmly knows what he wants and confident in his decision making. He has to be supportive, flexible, balanced and secure enough for me to run the race of life beside him. We must be supportive of one another! He must hold me in high esteem as his woman, his friend, his wife and his lover. Last but not least, he must be able to cover me, come rain or shine. When the climate changes, he must have tough skin to understand that storms are temporary conditions. We may have to walk out a few things, but we have variety, and strength; we are soul mates. There is no price too costly for us to pay to achieve our goals and dreams. We are a perfect fit for one another!

A Woman After Her Own Heart
will wait for her soul mate.
He will walk right into her life, perhaps
While she's purchasing shoes!

"What Lies Between Sisters"

Meet Leah: Leah was the elder sister, who loves her baby sister but her insecurity and doubts, not to mention her physical appearance, bothered her so Leah noted as tendered eyed and homely. Genesis 29: 17 but Rachael, whom you are about to meet, was beautiful and well favored. Poor Leah has to grow up under her youngest sister's noted beauty and favoritism. Leah didn't have a life coach assuring her that she had other qualities that Rachael did not possess. She didn't have an image consultant to give her a few beauty tips and positive affirmations of true beauty that was hidden. Leah just could not see past self-condemnation and her knowledge of being the oldest unmarried, and the least favored of the girls! A poor self-reflection created a desperate and lonely woman named Leah.

Meet Rachael: lovely as can be, well formed and youthful. Her appearance attracts the eyes of men and women. Rachael is spoiled but well liked and her doting family has made her feel secure and confident. Her exterior qualities have positioned her for love and marriage. Lucky Rachael, some might say if you have it flaunt it!

The Happening: Rachael meets Jacob, who falls head over heels with her, love at first sight. Jacob asks Rachael's father for her hand in marriage. Of course, her father agrees. During those times a marriage was arranged. Rachael's and Leah's father has a brilliant idea to get both girls down the aisle with the same man. His well-planned schemed worked and is still in progress today. Sisters are still willing to go down the aisle whether it is unmarriage bed or just down the movie theater aisle with her sister's man.

Leah knew that Rachael was Jacob's first choice, and she further knew that he had been deceived to lie with her. Could Leah have refused to be a plan that would leave her emotionally scattered, or did she agree because her biological clock was ticking? Can you image how Leah must have felt day in and day out that she married a man who loved her sister but he couldn't have her until he labored seven more years, for her a total of 14 years. Leah was deceived, much like the foolish thinking women of today, I have his baby and you don't. Leah bore his child but lived under the shadow of insecurity, fear, deceit, and a lower self-esteem than before she had his babies while her husband longed for her sister's hand! Proverbs: an unloved married woman, even the earth trembles. I am sure Jacob and the earth experienced many trembles!

How the earth still trembles today when two women share the same man, one has his lions and the other his heart: sisters sharing the same man and eventually the same bed. The second marriage between Rachael and

Jacob finally consummates the marriage with Rachael. I pray their sleeping quarters were far away from Leah's. What joy and pleasure when two people love one another. Rachael was the youngest sister, who must have been a child when Jacob met her, much like today's grown men who still have eyes for young women with a child's mind and a women's body.

<u>The Fireworks</u>: two sisters openly share the same man. Passion and desire was Rachael's and Jacob's atmosphere, and Leah had his babies. But now Rachael wants his babies too! Leah represents low self-esteem, low self-worth and a woman of age willing to settle under harsh circumstances. She has a man who lies next to her but his heart is at a different address. Rachael represents the woman who struggles to give birth to her dreams. She has the outer beauty but her inner self struggles with her inabilities and difficulties to bring fourth!

What lies between sisters besides the same man is the inability to tap into the consciousnesses of their deeper self, her womanhood her inner beauty, her intelligence, her dignity, her integrity. All those wonderful brand characteristics were never recognized. Each sister had the ability to say no, the ability to choose, just as today, ladies; you have the ability not to become unloved by the same man. You have the right to choose, and choose with dignity while maintaining a standard of being loved without compromise. What lies between sisters is self-hatred, an inability to love ourselves at all cost.

The Affair

I had an affair I was introduced and wooed by lyrics and sounds; I gave in to what I heard the affair began.

Conversations day and night I was influenced by intelligence. The descriptive nouns and verbs made my breathing so heavy leading me to inhale and exhale oh, ah, and sometimes why do I feel this way. As we paused with boldness we spoke of our affair and confessed our love to one another. I never felt guilty the emotion and passion I felt was indescribable. I took hold on to every sentence spoken with promise. We cherished every moment for we found ourselves renewing our vowels often. With confidence I spoke with eloquence. Words has been my lover and I his, for we speak well of one another. Learning and growing together he teaches and I speak the instruction, He is my why, my how, and the pronouns of my life. I love words for it was words that created my world!

Lesson Two: The Renaissance Woman

The Renaissance woman is the Rebirth and Revival of womanhood. She is a transitional movement, with expression.

Classical and influential giving beauty a new name she is the architectural mold. The Renaissance woman is the contemporary, yet she is the medieval using wisdom of all ages, capturing the minds of men. She is the formulation and arrangement of rules, creating harmony and balance. She is education, knowledge and proficient. Renaissance is the design in every woman waiting for expression of all ages!

Positive Words That Create Your World

Positive Words That Create Your World

_____

_____

_____

_____

_____

_____

_____

_____

_____

_____

_____

_____

_____

_____

_____

_____

_____

_____

_____

The Pages Have Turned!

I know that I deserve better, clearly it is understood I shall not want or need. Yet plagued experiences lead me astray.

Tears of sadness sometimes feelings of remorse drip down my face however each tear is an indication that I will cry no more!

Feeling creative, strong, fearless,
loving me loving you!
Resurrection comes!

The stream of life continues
with breaks and pauses.
The floods of mishaps and
misunderstandings and silent
communication, yet illusions never
prevail for imagination is greater.

Grace covers and change awaits
transition catapults me to a place
Called there.

Awakened by the inner man that
once knew how to love and be loved.
The mystery of cosmic love remains
hidden but still profoundly exists.

I journey to the next dimension of experience with no resistance, for love, and grace accompanies me!

The feminine presence of self
awareness and beauty awaken.
Simplified knowledge prevails. I journey!

The doors of the past have
been officially closed.
The entry way no longer exists!

This is a glorious page in my life, periods
of time, stages, phases, chapters, and
episodes have become a moment in time!
I finally realized to turn the pages
in my life was to just change
My mind!

Cry No More

Peace and Grace

*T*o all who read my book, I hope you enjoyed the humor the emotion and the journaling in this book. I write in hope that each woman will find herself on one of these pages and connect in some way. Hopefully you will heal, rejoice, and transform. Each story was written through experience or knowledge of others experiences.

Perhaps we will meet in life if not meet me through my writings, I have you in mind on every page. To meet you is only to meet myself!

Hello and Goodbye!

See you in the next book! Look for me on Facebook or email at ladiesfirstworldwide@gmail.com or visit the website Ladiesfirstseminars.com. Loving you as I love myself!

Glenda Rose

Love Always Glenda Rose